You are a body
worthy of representation
in Literature and Art.

Love and light
to you
my dear reader.

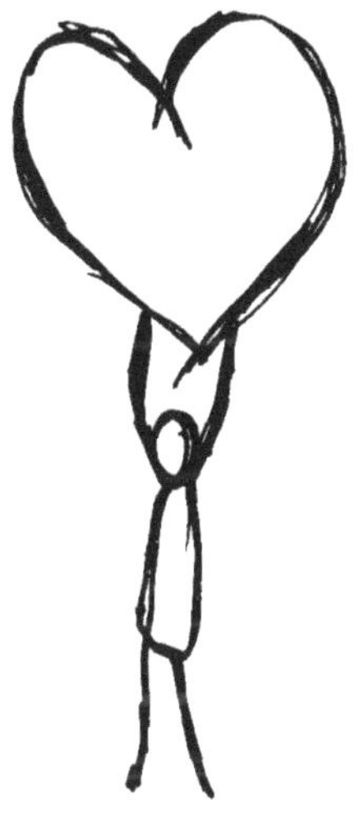

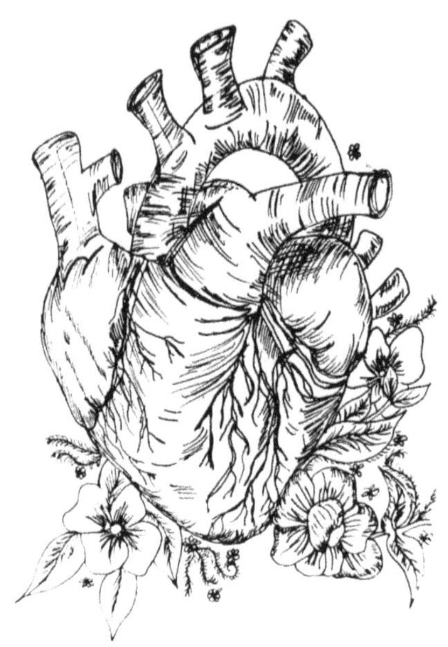

Here I shall be.

Milk-flowers fall on sheets of thin ice,
wavelet tear drops of dew rest on pink buds,
translucent rims of yellow light,
purple lavender fuzz faints onto white pillows,
drops of melting pendant spears
disappear into peach lotus puddles.
We make clouds in the air with young breath.
Candied ginger and roasted tangerines
light warm rain starts to feather down
sweet vanilla air turns silver condensation
sticky and patterned like fresh string pluck,
cobwebs shining in the sun.
Frosty crushed ice falls apart,
delicate rings ripple across streams of spring water,
cool and earthy, petals like eyelids, soft and lined,
tasselled willow amulets,
like angel hair pasta woven intricately,
yet so effortlessly.
Milk-flowers fall on sheets of thin ice.
If you need to find me, here I shall be.

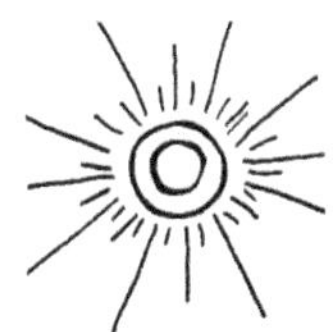

Prayer

At the back of the house there was a wet stone temple,
dew from the over-hanging banana leaves,
dripped down hydrating beds of algae,
white lotus flowers decorated the shrine
and scented the damp bubble of air that hovered
over it.
A coconut saffroned and stained red, another cut in half, milk
white.
A deity, black stone idol, peaceful and natural.
There was something so calm about this little world.
Hidden in the back of an unregistered home,
upheld by the offerings of venerations,
apples and oranges, childhood prayers, clapping hands,
pink nail buds.
Ghee lamps, thick sunflower, golden soaked in holy thread,
whilst lavender incense sticks burned out,
and fell into piles of soft grey ash.
A cross banded with light blue sits
beside a Virgin Mary key-chain.
They lie against the walls of the Ganesha house.
They remind me of you.
Regular replacements of fresh Marigolds,
and matches, wax candles were scattered about.
I have gotten into the habit of praying for you.
Maybe when it rained I realised how different the droplets
tasted, impure and troubled.
The rain there seemed clear like spring,
trustworthy and kind.
Maybe some things need to change, and maybe I need to say
thank you.
But for now I spend my time praying for you.
But maybe all I'm actually doing is praying for myself.

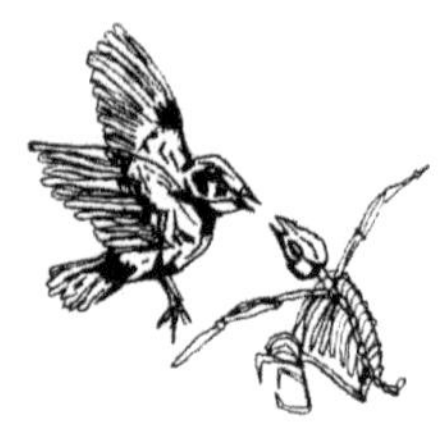

Bare bones

What was longing to be said furrowed
into bruises around the throat,
weighs heavy on the rib cage,
breathing becomes shallow.
Everyday,
trying to keep the bare bones covered
under stretched withered skin,
desperate to come out,
pierce out of the flesh,
and reveal the truths buried deep within.
Come out with it
or let it consume,
denature sparks of life
and ultimately break out from the body.

Sugar Cane Hair

Dusty sugar cane hair matted dry by the sun
sways in the warmth of a fruity air
salted by sea water.
Slap stings like a summer mosquito bite.
'Ayyy Matlo' Creole spills over smooth like a pink
glass of tapioca milk, cold creamy,
touching the ripped flesh of my lip.
Dry lips, Indian skin, pink lips, full lips.
It's the season for hot sticky chilly honey
lathered on stinging pineapples,
coconut gateaux, Pork dim sum,
glass cherries, drops of condensation beading,
slipping
down.

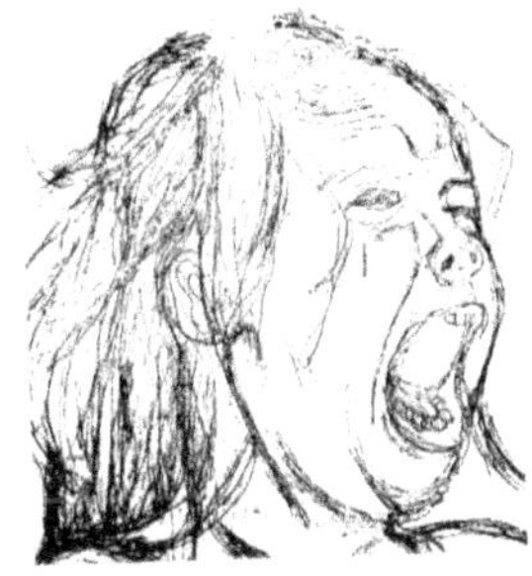

Blood from my ear soaks into my yellow Dodo T-shirt.
I can taste it.
Selling outside Phoenix market,
I buy the pink flip flops, light blue bands, rubber smell.
One size fits all.
I sit by the sea watching the fish fly
and the fire flies drops dead.
Crusted drops of blood dotted on my neck.
I breathe in and walk into the water.
Dusty sugar cane hair matted
softens like vermicelli.
I walk and walk.
I am never coming back.

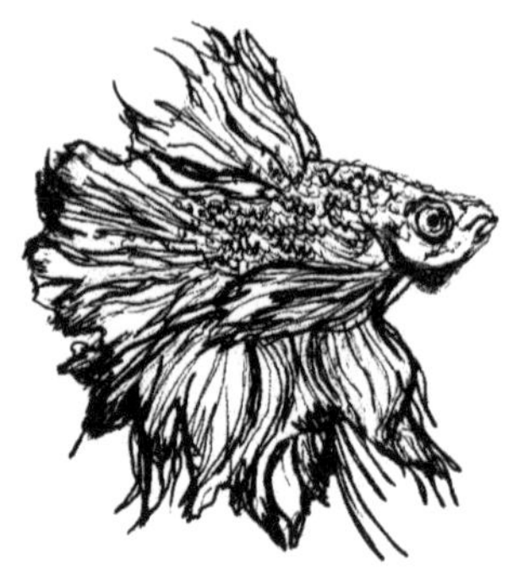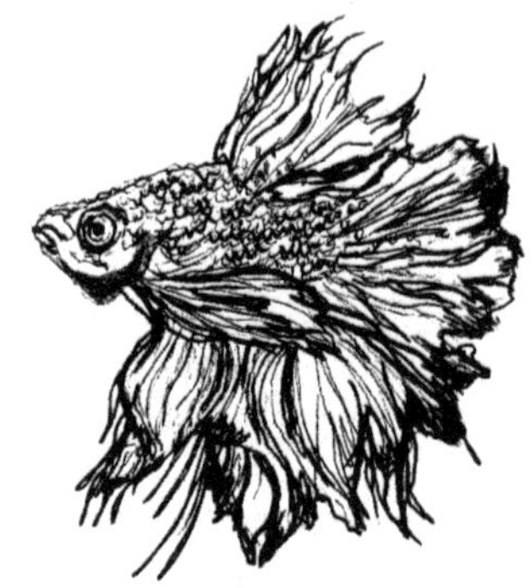

Angel fish

Angel fish, watery ridge, it dissolves away
my hands in your hands.
Pink lotus buds,
lemon paper cuts.
You fade away into the sea.
Shiny scales blue cobalt,
tired of being dull.
Blunt endings I fish out from bright beginnings.
I cannot drown,
You cannot swim.
Angel hairs floating,
softening, tasselled flows,
dreaming away from delicate love prose.
You forget.
Maybe never retained in the first place.
Ruptures in motion,
big waves, harsh rhythms, sorry.
Angel fish, watery ridge, it dissolves away
my hands in your hands.
Pink lotus buds,
lemon paper cuts.

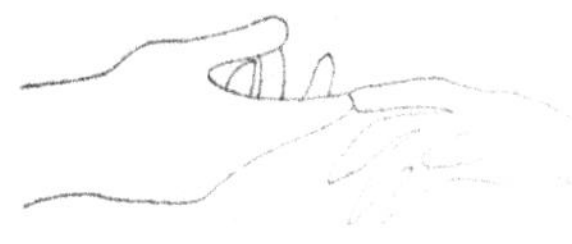

Sweetness

Dream of the sweetness,
thick Puit D'amour custard saffron yellow.

Hands feel dry.
In the kitchen a fresh box,
the finest in Phoenix.

As if a blue marlin gulping down sea water mackerel.

Run the tongue across the ripples of custard like a
natural.

Scoop the syrup soaked cherry.
Mouth mouths.

The sweetness sickly wonderful,
sticky and messy,
Cockerel pecking at the garden shed,
And the bamboo chair creaking as it swings.

You finished her Puit D'amour.
A lizard swings down from the ceiling and pokes his
tongue out.

The custard, the cherry, the shortbread biscuit.
Finished.
My favourite.
Crying hands look empty.

'Would you like mine ?'
Throws up blue confetti.
Favourite Puit D'amour cakes.
I reach for my phone and Google the recipe.

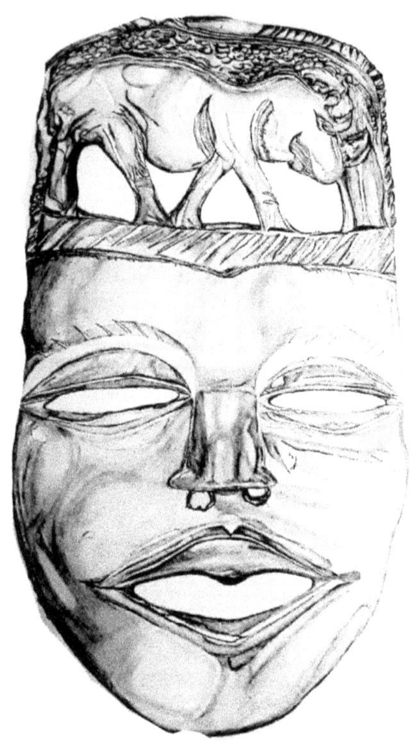

Brown skin

Splashes of rain make the air thick with humidity.
It's sugar cane season, sponge brown air.

Dug nail deep powdered savat,
an itchy cut on your right toe.
It hurts but feels good to rub it on the ground.
Red clay softens becomes slippery.

Dip your fingers in the metal tin of dry Milo.
Lick them first so it sticks.
Malted chocolate brown like your hair, like my skin.

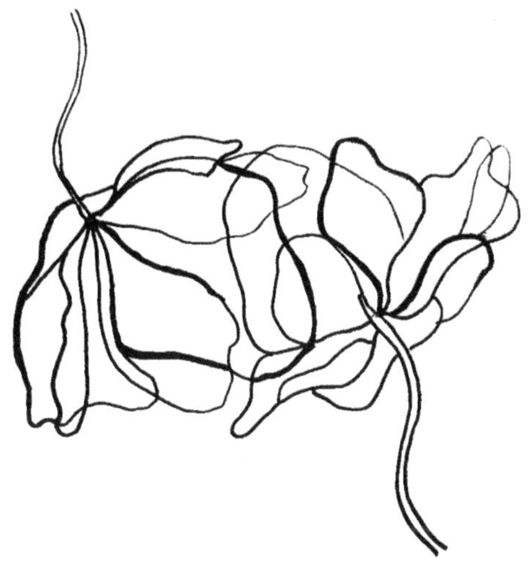

Milo tin

I miss the Cabin biscuits with thick salted butter.
Dip them in vanilla Bois Cheri.

Assemble the blue gas tanks rusted iodine.
The roll of the drum beats too loud.
The voice is too bellowing.

The water feels shallow, cool and complacent.
Tie dye water weaves greens with white light,
it looks blue.

The smell of damp is somehow fresh here.
Our veins are blue, but yours are purple.
I tell you my eyelid has been beating
by itself for a while.

Tap the temple to the beat of the song.
I laugh. You tap my temple. Tap, tap, tap.
It still blinks. I go in for a second dip.
My Milo tin is running out.

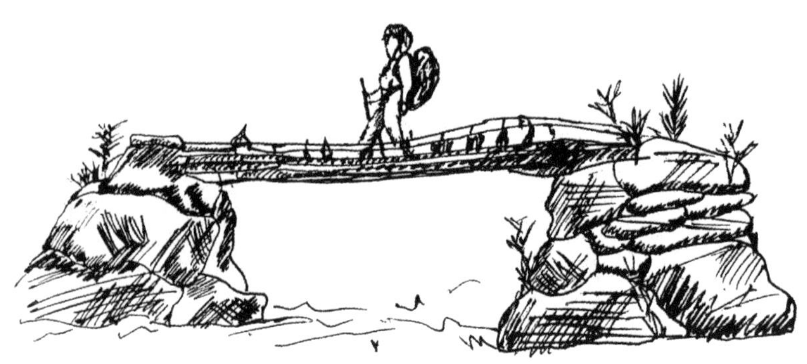

Carrier

How do I carry your story forward
without appropriating ?
Without having my own stories displace
your accounts,
without drawing attention to my pain,
my own train of thoughts ?
I will do my best to honour
your honesty
and above all
deliver with love.

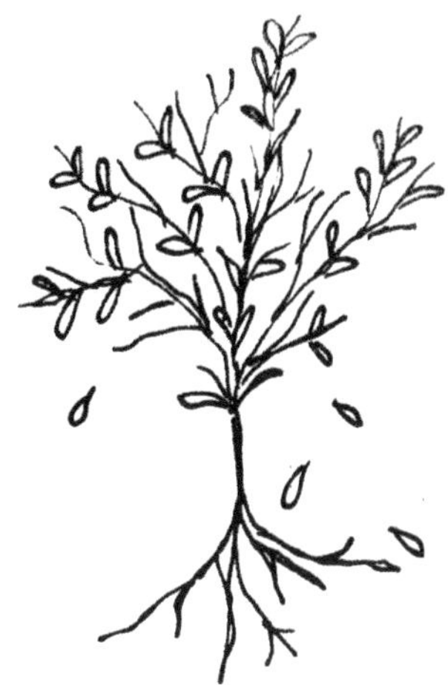

Falling, changing.

The leaves have fallen.

The trees are bare.

As I stare at the snow covered ground.

Regardless of the time that has passed.

I still haven't
        forgotten you.

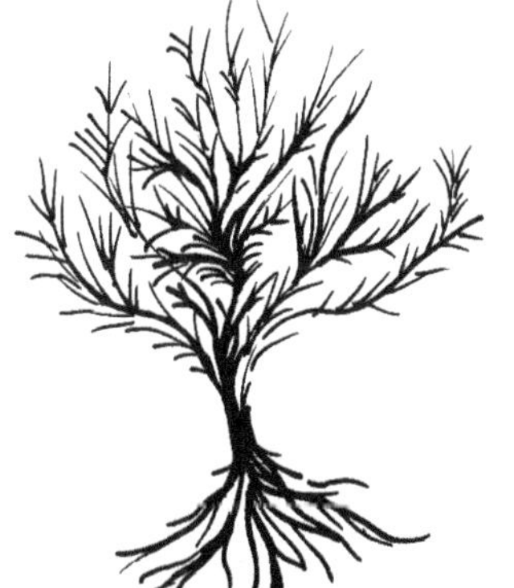

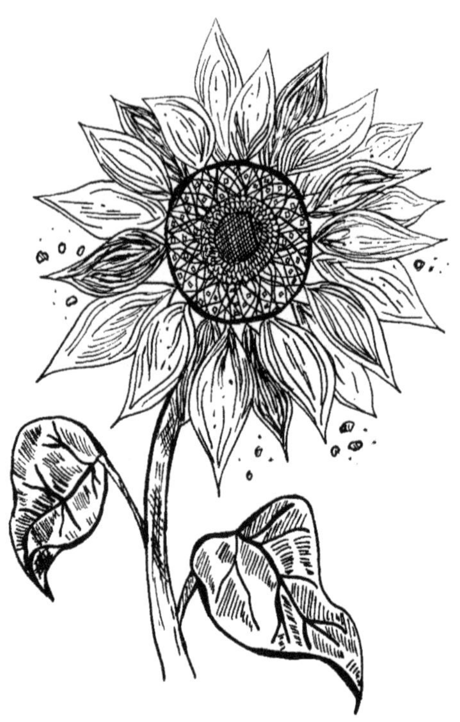

Days

Day breaks and I realise I am back where I started.

You are not here and I am so lost.

All I can do is think about you.

I'm too used

to having you be a part

of my day.

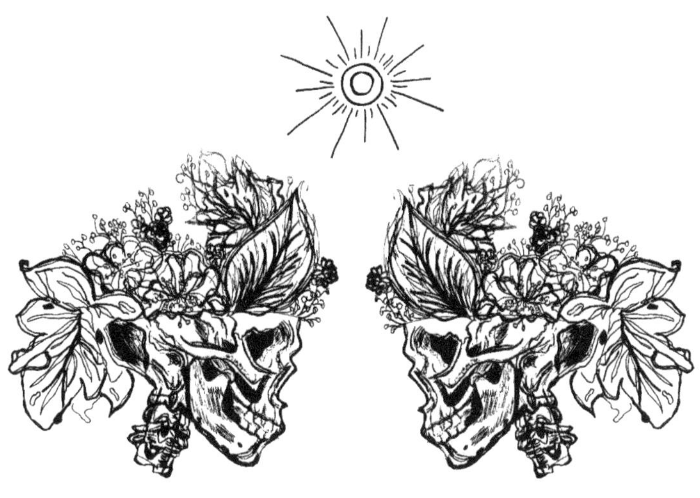

Phantom limb.

Like a phantom limb
I feel you in my presence.

My blood mixes with your honey,
the socket longs for vessels.

The veins long for a blood line,
imagination mockingly teases.

Construct bone and muscle out of thin air.
Infuse sensation and motion.

Then laugh as I realise
there is nothing there.

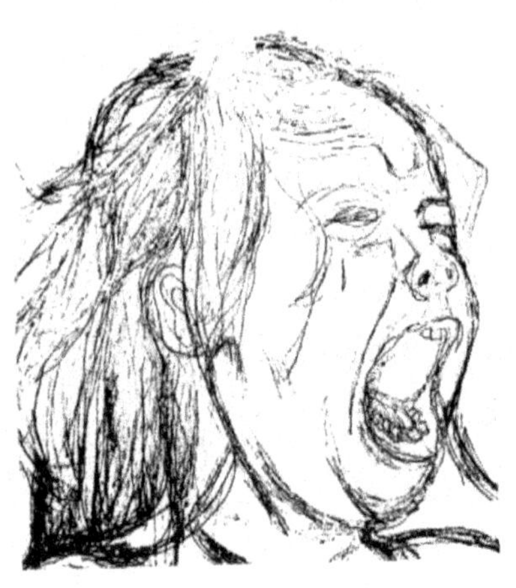

Mango syrup

Sticky mango syrup drips
down the chin.

Flakes of crushed ice
under the beating yellow.

We run in the dust,
elbows dry
wide eyed.

Funny songs.
A curl hangs down.

Dried up gecko salted by the sun.
Biscuits with butter,
an egg turned over tank
water.

Full tea leaves boiled frothed milk.
Your hands are big.
Laughing, tears roll into ear drums.
Upside down.

Red marble floor, cold smells like old cotton. It has
melted into a puddle by the hand.

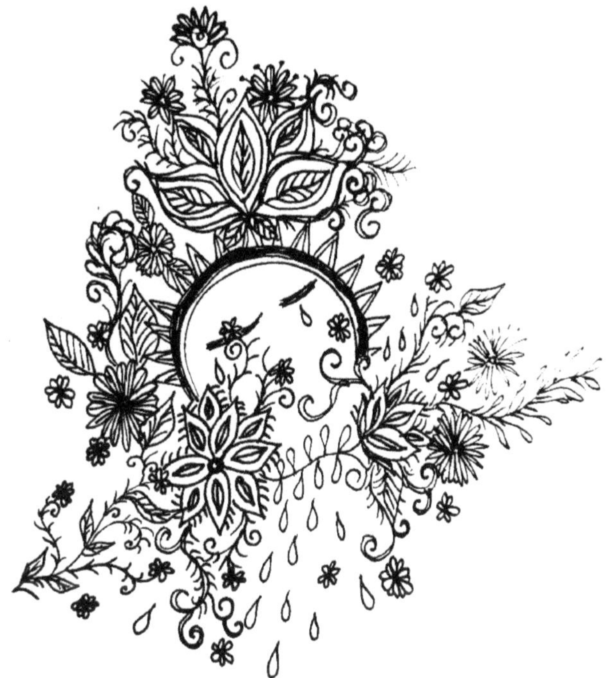

History

When I was younger I was called brown.
Primary colour impaired.
Puzzled in me frustrations.
Where are you from ?
Complicated histories of hostility,
moving bodies,
circling migration, indentured systems,
Creole, Chinese, Indian linguistic creations,
 from French invasions and British colonisation.
Mango pickle honey sickle.
Fate is pathetic and fickle.
Long eyelashes black beauty spot below the lip.
Chilly soup, an inbred group.
No concept for me, no room for me.
Dodo key chain and pink milk in the sun,
sweat moustache and pink tongues.
Beautiful island rum white leaf.
Vanilla pod and breezy seas.
Thank you for the pain and burden,
for now I have a voice and one that will not silence.

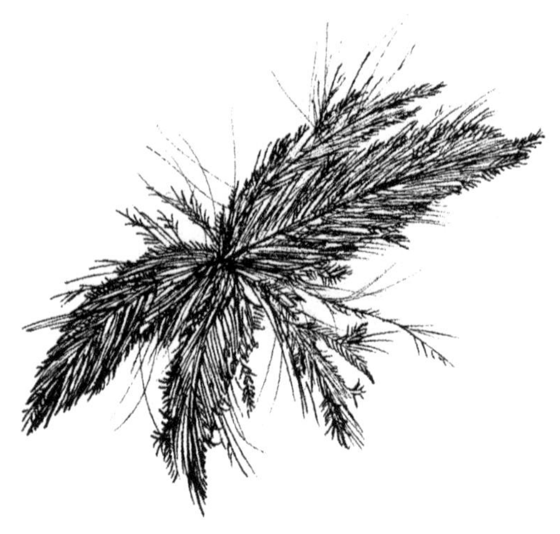

Watercress Soup

Watercress soup. Bouillon Brede.
Warm watery base, splashes of olive oil,
and soft pat leaves
of limp cress float,
so heavy yet so light,
as if all the stresses that burdened
its thin limbs,
from being plucked from the ground,
washed and violated, had disappeared.
Soaked straight into its tiny green muscles,
drowned away into the heat of the water.
Surrender to its fate at the hands of a higher source.
Its leafy starchy life,
burned out, cooked until numb.
But somehow still tastes sweet.
It the best kind of soup
for a rainy day.

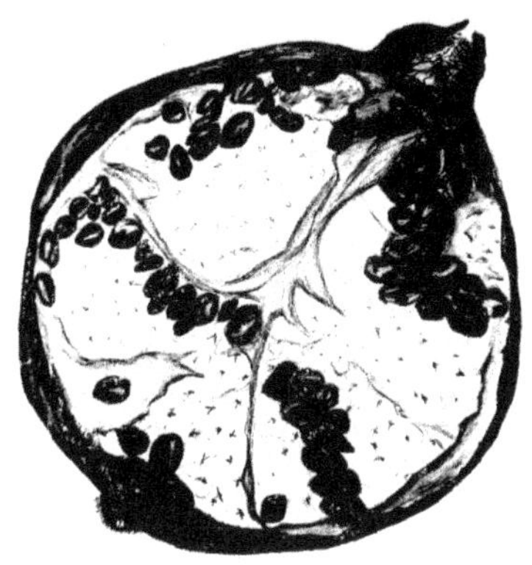

Fluorescent

Sun tan lotion, purple speckled light,
dotted fluorescent.
The pink flakes of your skin disappear into the fluorescent.

Standing stagnant, blue lights flashing.
I was sure I did not drink.
I was besotted by the fluorescent.

My room hot and sticky
no air,
shiny buzzing flies, blood was sweated,
fluorescent.

The neon drinks we guzzled
matched the colour of her headband knotted
fluorescent.

Beads of sweat on top of your lip
as you scream in pain.
The veins in your eyes scrunch, I blotted away
the fluorescent.

Recall the way you nervously tapped your thumbs
and wring your jaw,
immersed all in light
spotted fluorescent.

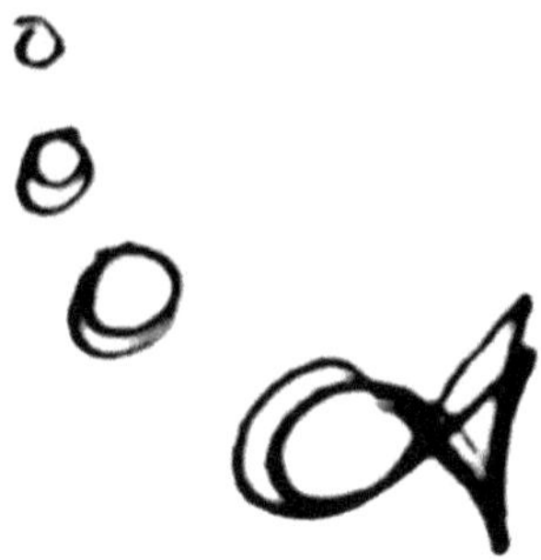

Pungent

In the market
I always remember the strong smell
of salted fish.
Dry bone,
spine dehydrated
fermenting in the sun,
pungent strong, as fresh
bunches of coriander bounded by blue
bands dripping robin water,
rests a level below.
A mango stall opposite
sells both fresh and pickled,
red spice soaked
crushed ice fresh.

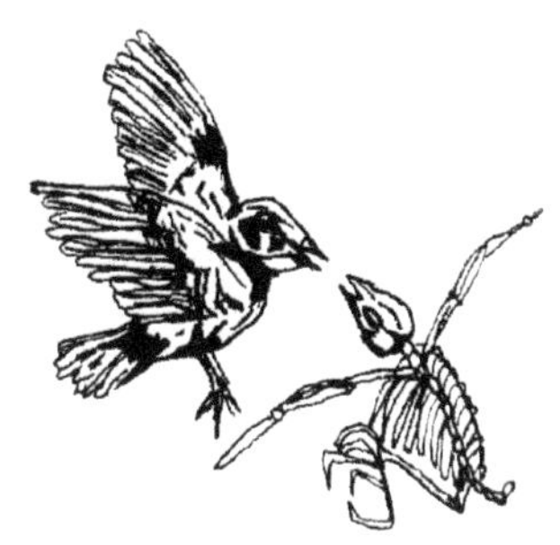

New beginnings

After the wings were clipped,
and the feathers frayed,
for a split second I saw
the pillars of my boing,
the carbon of my body,
the moments that made the skeleton
and upheld the turbulence
of my temporal life.
It was beautiful.
Just for a second.
Beautiful.
Second gone.
Flesh falls, the soul has left
and the vertebrae
comes undone like bobbins
of white thread stacked
knocked over ricochet down
like hard rain.
Falling into pillows
of soft willow.
Goodbye to the light
I once knew.

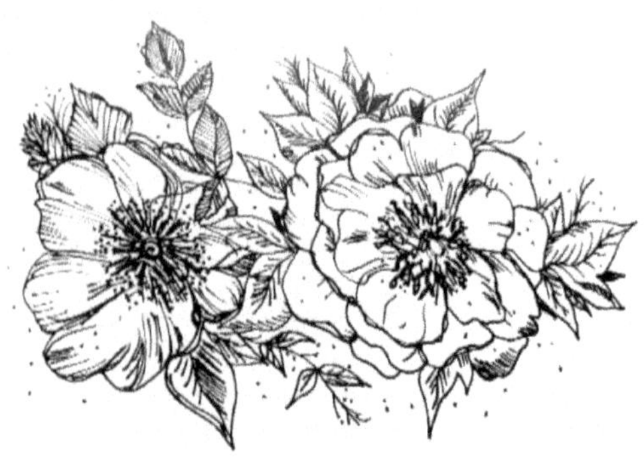

Ghee lamps lit in the rain,
place them on the wet footsteps
lined up to the doorway.
Rose water, dry chillies, fruit flies, mango pickle.
I smell the salt
of the seaweed.
The sweetest sugar cane kept
for about a week or so,
big flowers on big skirts,
Sega music dancing
to the roll of the drum
and the blaze of the fire.
The sea foaming white and warm
washes the translucent crabs,
tiny and scuttling as if dancing,
to the song sung by the descendants
of indentured labourers
over years of mustard sun golden dripping.
Heat rashes and coriander coated finger tips,
green.
Who needed a knife ?
The fresh leafy branches,
rip it.
Like you ripped me.
patter of dog paws,
Rolling in the red dust of clay soil.
Spirited with the rays.

Rain

Do you remember the rain there ?
It was not like in London.
Excuse my wet hair.
It gets really curly.
When it rained there it was yellow.
Santa Barbara.
It smelled different,
like sand and soil.
I'm sorry.
Here the rain smells like metal and cardboard.
And you.
Your smell, I miss here.
You always had this wide smile, tiny indentations
on your face.
You want something to eat ?
I have peanut cookies.
It's simple and sweet, but I guess it's okay.
So the rain you were saying ?
No, no I was saying.
Used and damp washed cotton
fraying at the earthy water droplets.
It was calm.
I see you many times a day.
My favourite part of the day.
Its funny because you chose to no longer exist
for me.
Sorry my hands feel sweaty.
Mouth is a little fuzzy.
Tea ?
I still like it here.
Its in my bones I guess.
But I can also leave and not look back for a long time.
Sugar and milk ?

Fine lines

There was a chance to repair
the fine lines, the fine hair.
Can you stop asking what day it is ?
We'll never be able to get through this.
People were sitting still and the waves
that washed passed us reminded me
of when we were kids
cold green glass and hard water.
I punch your ribs.
I might decide to leave but before I go,
did you steal my sunglasses ?
The one's with pink stars
plastic crystal rims.
Give me something sweet like sugar cubes
with almonds and green raisins.
Please stop crying.
But I cannot.
I can feel it.
I don't feel it.
Maybe. Lie. Maybe 12, 13.
Maybe years now.
Tepid water now.
Something simple. How ?
'You'll be fine.'
Hahaha. How do you know ?
I'm going to run in the rain for a while.
You can have it your way.
Don't buy the blue ones remember.
Long day.
I love you.
See you soon.

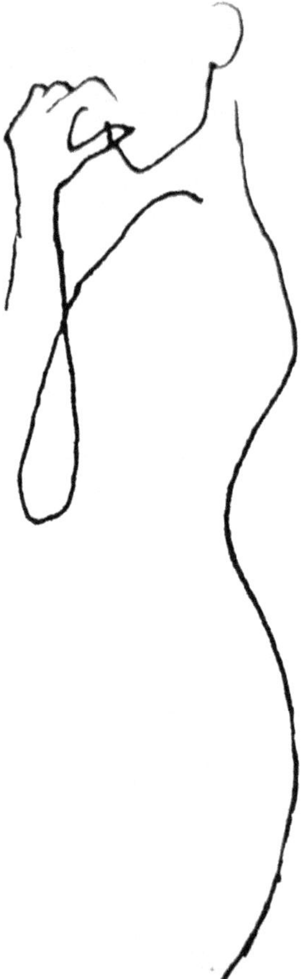

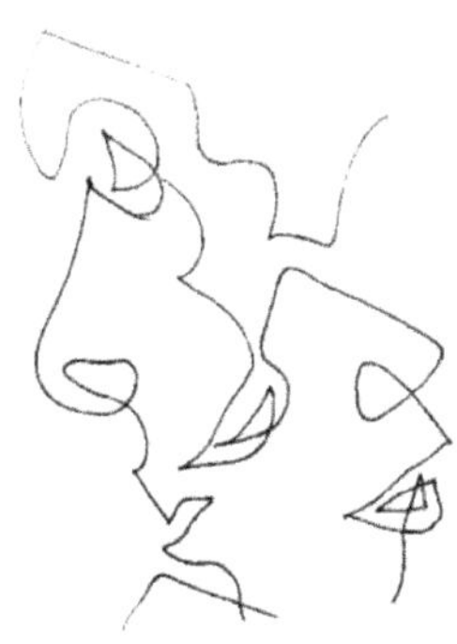

Good game

It seemed it was too easy
to learn the language of validation
yet so difficult to understand
the language of self love.
There exists sweet moments.
Honey pure and happy,
only to be combed over
by feelings of insecurities.
They allowed mistreatment
and coldness.
They tolerated belittlement from a boy
who did not understand how to address a friend's
emotions.
They allowed sadness and longing.
You played a good game.

Touch, coming and going.
Hoping to change destiny.
Meant to be.
Just because we touch doesn't mean I love you.
Touch, coming and going.
I miss another soul,
so mine is weathered,
which are the frays you have to love.

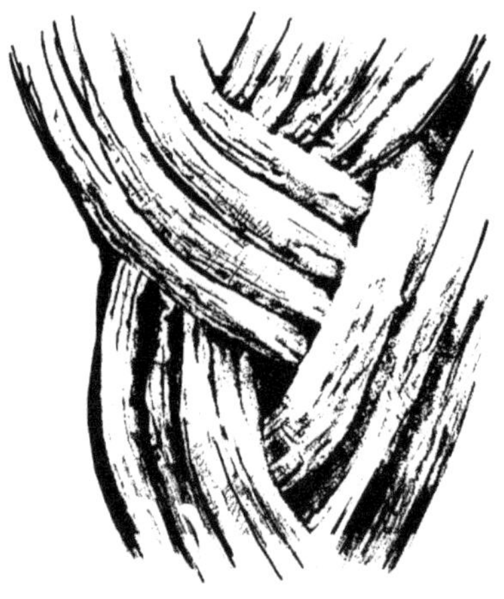

Touch, coming and going.
The rhythm of being broken
is becoming a tune
that I am starting to feel comfortable with.
Let it play on a little longer.
I wish we touched.
I fell in love with you without feeling your skin.
Lets move.

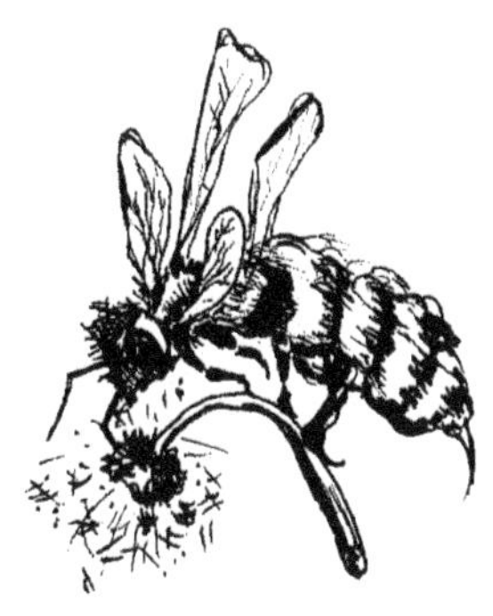

Nature

There are ways of thinking and behaving that abide by nature.
Like how the honey bee seeks
nectar from the hearts of flowers
that give sweet dew
to the hands of man,
or the woman who holds the hand of her lover because she
feels home.
If that is the right and only way
then I am afraid to admit
that I am not human,
for I feel things I cannot explain
and for too damn long.
And do things that have no reason.
I guess
that makes me unnatural.

Messy bedroom thoughts.

There's a Snickers wrapper under my bed.
Dum dum dum la la la.
Ball of micellar soaked cotton.
I'm lying on the carpet
staring at the ceiling.
It feels okay.
In the quiet.
You don't think so far ahead huh ?
A wave passes over us.
Everywhere purple.
Pointed player.
Whistling trumpet.
Let's dance.
I want cold water on my back.
Do you try on your clothes like this ?
Do you always eat your apples like this ?
All the peeling leaves.
Green chlorophyll.
Smells unnatural.
Do you remember ?
Whatever comes around lets promise to laugh.
Round faces.
You love tantrics even if you don't know it.
Ouch.
I like that song.
La la la la.
I don't think I care.
Money child.
Do you want to sit on the roof.
Icy shower head.
The light has gone out.
But I have a candle on the desk
and a match in the jewellery box.

Joy

Is

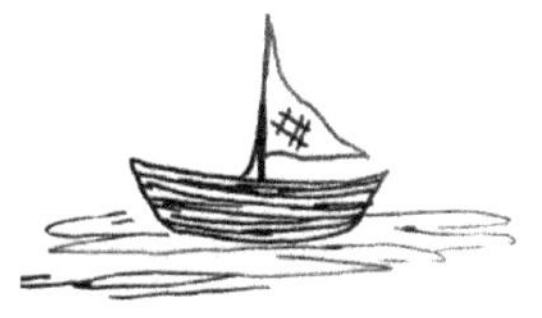

Fluid.

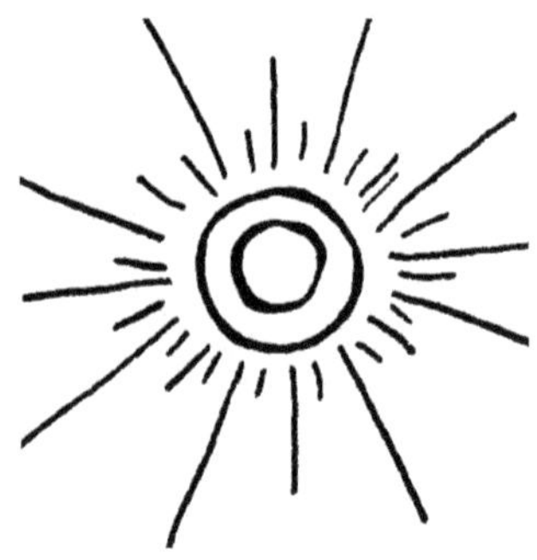

Love

I think today is the first time I understood love.
It is not selfish.
It is not spiteful.
It is one of the only things in our consuming world
that is pure and beautiful.

It is funny and sweet,
completely trustworthy.
It is completely doing something
for someone else,
because you feel whole when you do.
It is the jasmine flower
that keeps you breathing when you are in a coma.

It is the one that hides the bullet
from the gun,
spreads their touch across the heart,
like when the sun touches the skin.

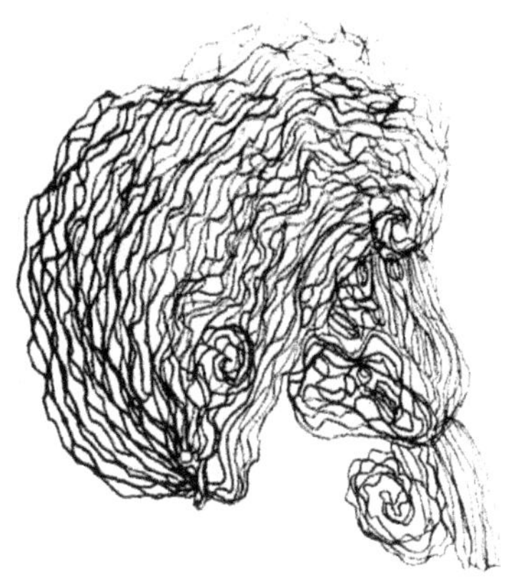

I feel as if I have been living a really superficial life.
I need to breathe and be one with myself
and others around me.
I want to be happy.
I want to love and be loved.
It's not about the nicest clothes
Or cars or houses
Or showing off.
Its about smiling with your heart
and living with
love and laughter.

Forever and Always

Know that in me
you will always
have someone
who
loves you.

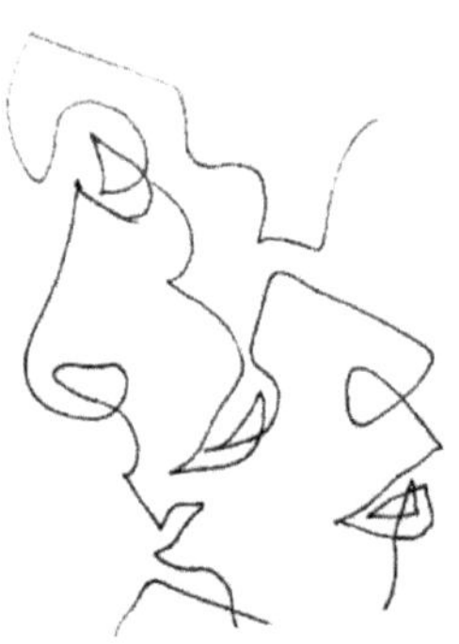

Missing you.

I shall take your leave now,
for I have done my job in giving you light again,
now with your blessing
 I
       fade
                away
into
         the flames.

Promise me
               two things.
Love yourself,
and visit my memory
                every now

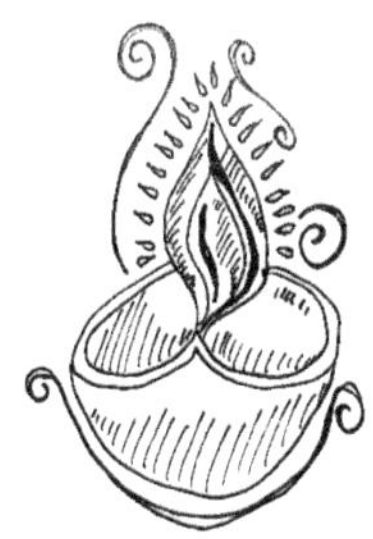

and again.

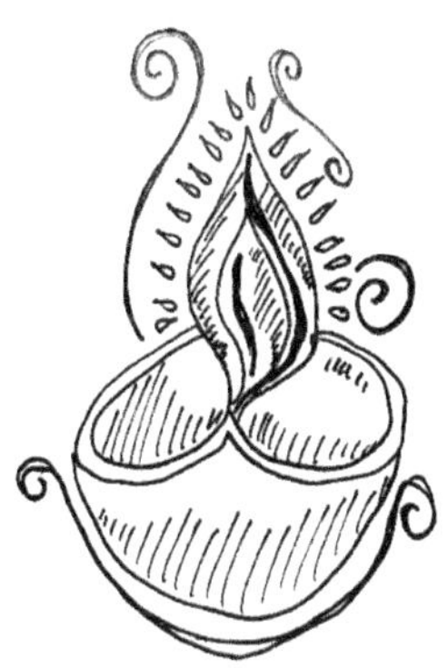

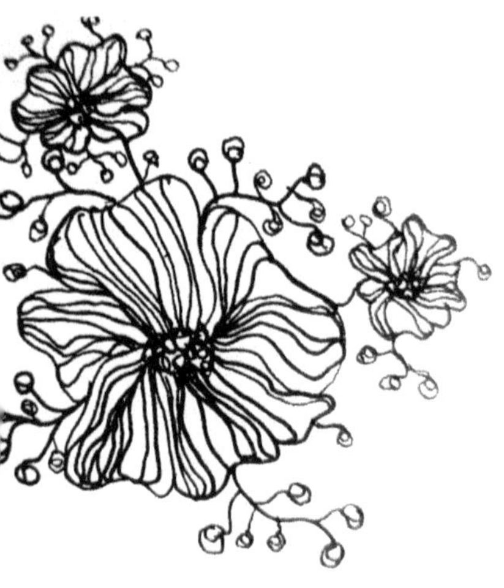

Tell me what I did.

I love how absolutely kind you are to others.
I get that you didn't like me that much,
but you were so kind to everyone else.

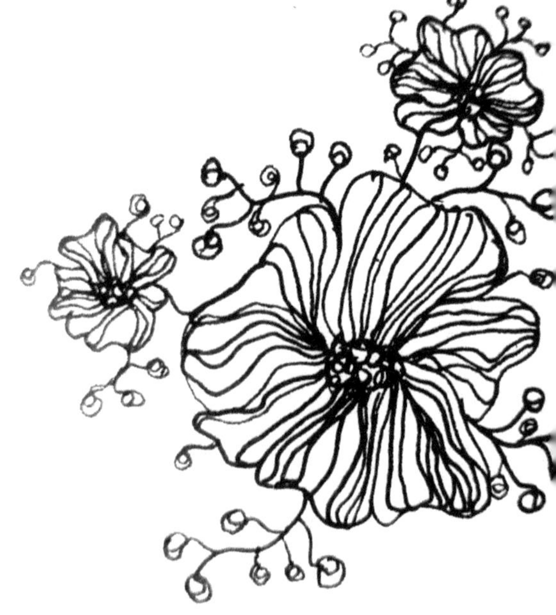

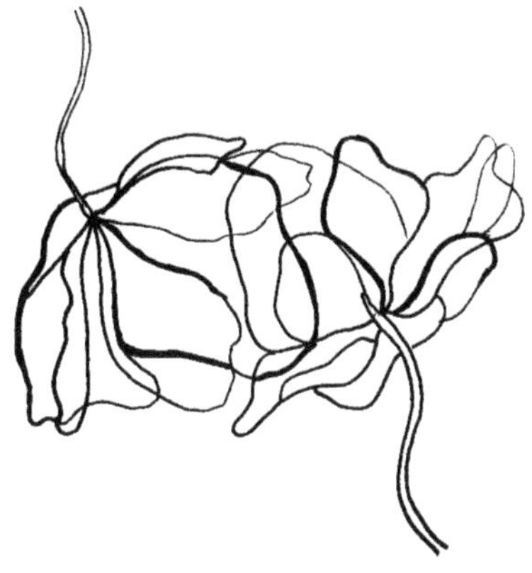

Pathetic love.

Part of me knows that you were aware
that I had a soft spot for you,
and so I would do pretty much anything to help you out.

I let you use me
because in a way I felt closer to you.
Then when it came to saying goodbye
to a friend,
you treated everyone else
with kindness and wouldn't even let me hug you.

You made me feel as if
you were disgusted by me.
I've never felt that way before.

It broke my heart, and the clincher is
I still love you,
and would probably come running
if
you ever needed me again.

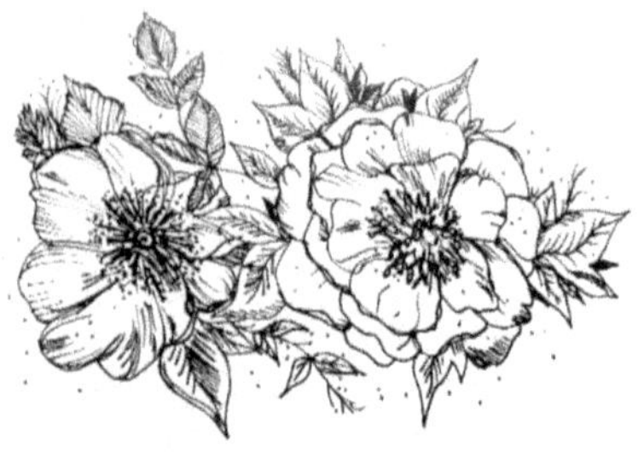

The moon and your cheek

When I was a child I was told of a tradition
of kissing someone on the cheek
when you see a full moon.
You are supposed to make a wish
and the act is said to bring you luck.
As an adult my foolish heart
now spends every night talking to the moon,
alone,
missing you,
hoping that you are somewhere looking up
at the same moon,
and that somehow connects us.
Even just for the briefest of moments.

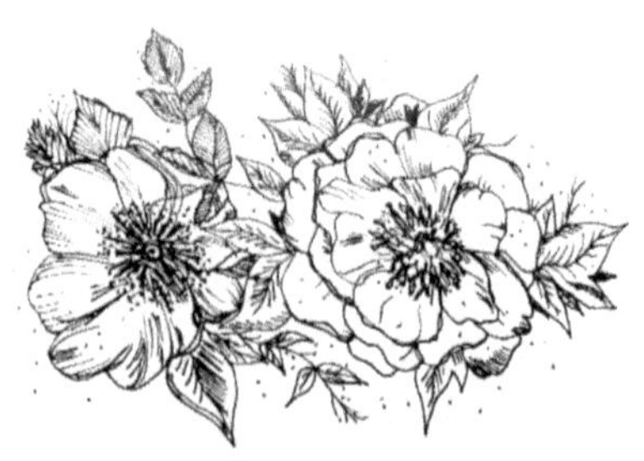

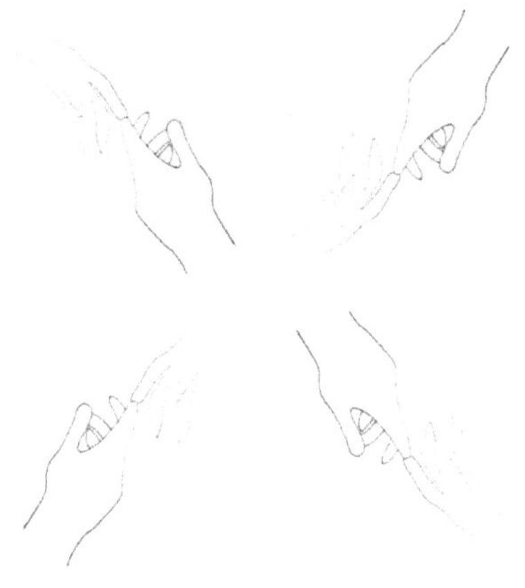

I guess I have been falling apart
ever since we said goodbye.
I tried to pretend life was good and move on.
But your smile has imprinted onto my heart.
Soon we won't be here,
so I told you how much you meant to me.
And you said nothing.
And so
I continue
to
fall
apart.

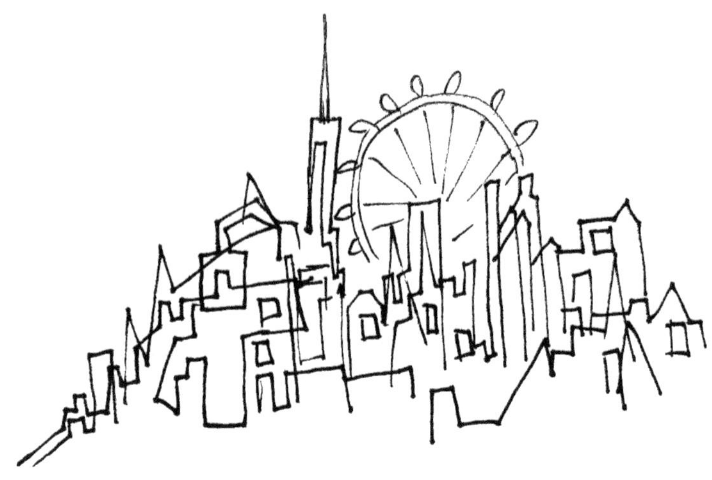

London

There is something about the smoke,
the grime,
the rain,
the messy medicated twists,
of the dingy streets
that I am absolutely
in love with.
Perhaps it is the fact that for all
its apparent surface
of dirt and rudeness,
it is home to all
and closed to none.

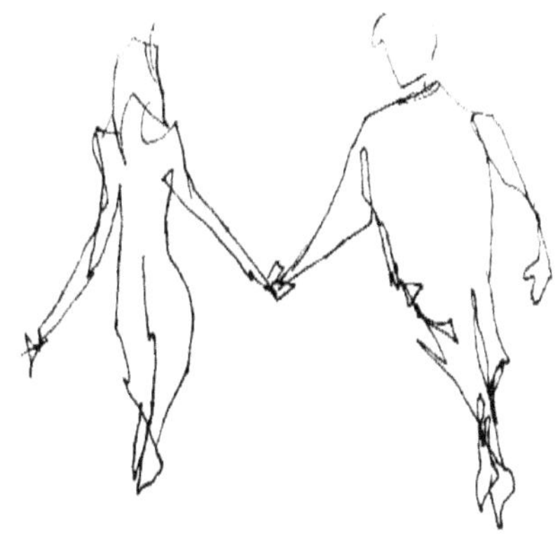

Snow

When I think of you
I think of snow.
I see you as insanely
beautiful.
Pure.
But like the snow
you melt away.
Never saying goodbye.
Never looking back.
And never caring about the
damage
you left behind.
And just like snow,
despite how cold
and destructive you
can be, you are still so
incredibly beautiful
to me.

When you decide
to look back,
if you ever do,
I'll still be here
waiting to hold
your hand.
Waiting for it to start
snowing again.
Waiting to catch ice drops
on my tongue.
I know our time will be the
same.
I will fall into you
desperately in love
and you will melt away
without acknowledging our
world.

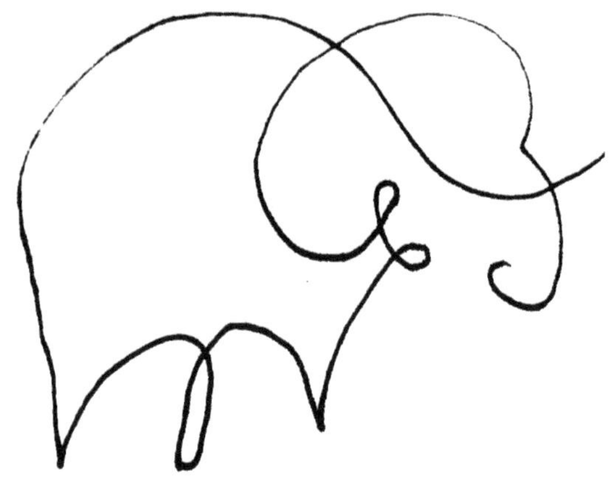

Faith

It left without a trace,
thin faith became thinner,
trickling rivers didn't satisfy like they use to.
Memory
like a string
is fraying,
and the rain keeps on falling,
washing the mud away.
Maybe its a good thing that I remember
and then let go with grace.

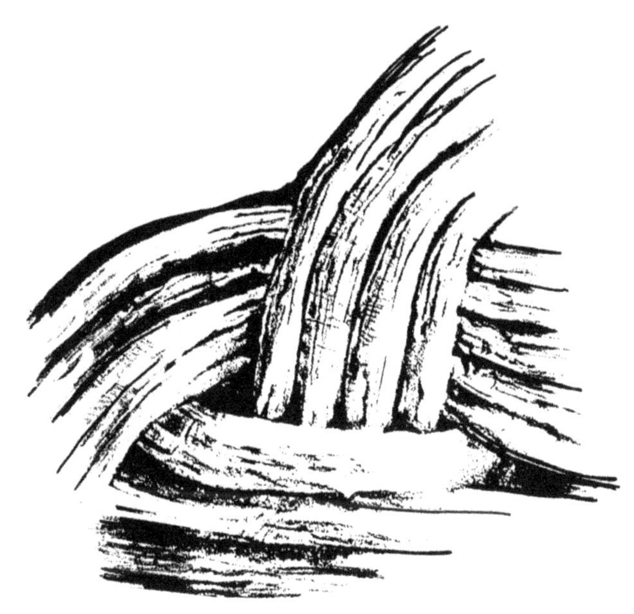

Learnt and learning

Blood ties
and age old generational lies
seem to bound us
to specific situations or ideas.
They programme our sense of the world
in ways we are only starting to understand.
Clip them and you start to see
things in a different light.
You may choose to return
or choose to change
and pass on what
you have learnt.

Dear You,
I haven't much to share, nor much to say, for if I give you the
answers you may never bare the scars that teach you of the deceit
and judgement the world will pour into you. Like salt in an open
wound, like lemon on a fresh paper cut, it will sting, you will bleed
and bruise, and cry and scream, and continue to fall and fall, until it
seems there is only darkness. But the one piece of advice I do have
for you is that all of this pain, all of this hurt, all of these storms,
will transform you, build you, teach you of your incredible worth,
that is beyond the physical realms. You are a spiritual power, beaten
and knocked over, but powerful and strong, and above all the
ultimate survivor. Have courage in your convictions, stand by your
mistakes, love every bump and imperfection, every unsymmetrical
line of overstretched flesh, look at yourself in the mirror and see
what I see. A beautiful strong human being who will forever fight.
Carry love in your heart, carry passion, never align your worth
with that of another, or change to fit the ideal of another. Protect
your energy and be not afraid to love, for love from you is a gift
from the highest light.

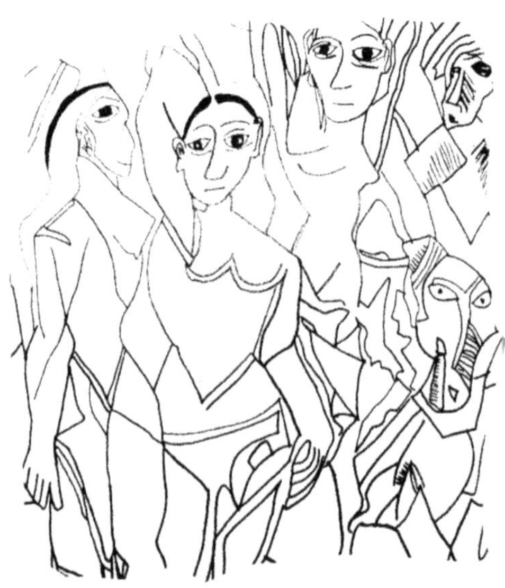

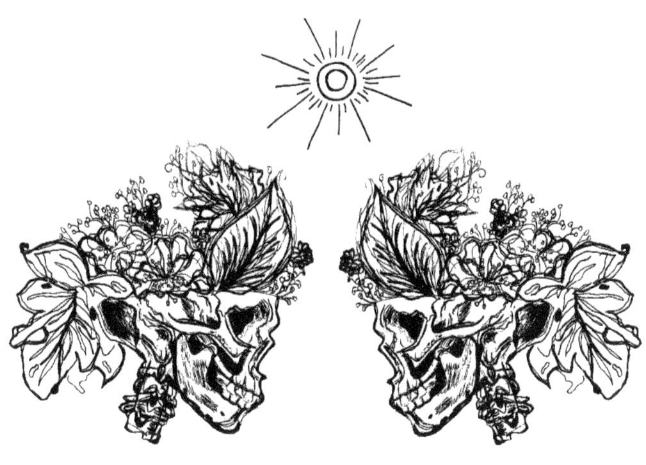

King's College London morning.

The sleep derived
caffeinated city slicker
coin ridder
day dreamer
carrying natural romances of the 1800's.
Cobble steps across the grey bustling streets
of Strand in heels rushing past the needy,
begging by Holborn station,
and bankers filing into HSBC
clutching onto morning coffees,
adjusting ties.
Earphones tangle,
cold air hits the unscathed face
of the free thinker
rushing to a morning meeting
with Ghosh and Ishiguro.

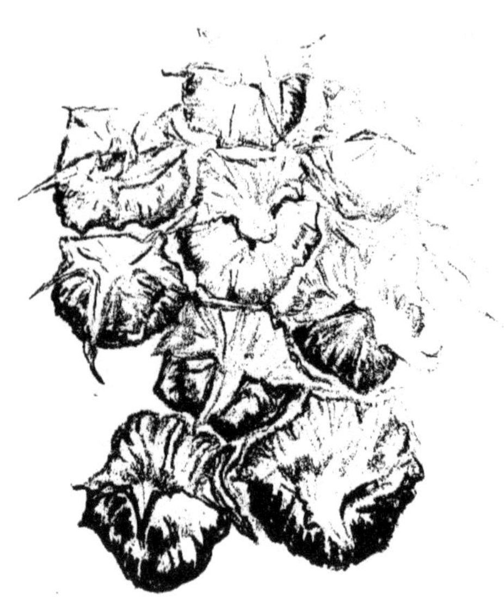

Pineapples and red buses.

There is a strange world that has been created,
where the neon flashing lights,
of red buses
carry islanders
who buy imported pineapples
and wear winter coats.

Who work to survive
in an environment
that has told them time
and time again
that they do not belong.

Yet they continue to stride
forward with the cold
air hitting their faces and the sun
in their hearts.

Holding onto the hands
of their young, bright children.
Do not be fooled.
this is your home too.

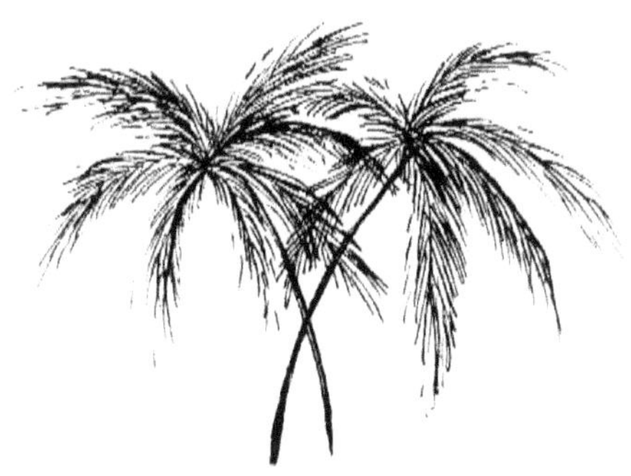

Memories from Phoenix

There is a small shop
at the corner of Campbell road
in Phoenix, Vacoas,
that sells about five batteries,
stickers, screwdrivers,
wet newspapers damaged from the orange rain,
lucky dip scratch cards and stale biscuits
slathered in thick pink icing.
It is run by a woman who looks about 500 years old.
Every morning she sits on an unbalanced,
dingy wooden stool
and chews on sugar cane whist no one
walks into her store.
Yet she smiles,
constantly waving at children riding their bikes
and lost tourists using Google maps.
She spits out the sugar cane fibres
onto the road and wipes her hands
on her dress.
Another good day of business.

Sweet rain

The morning rain
cold and fresh,
pours down,
hitting the sun which makes the air
smell of sweet pineapples.

I rush down the hallway
drying my hair,
pistachio flannel fraying towel,
barefoot and smiling,
faded blue.

I hear the neighbours
splashing water on their porches
cleaning the night's labour.

The birds begin to sing
whilst the rain splashes
Sweet hums
become softer
and softer.

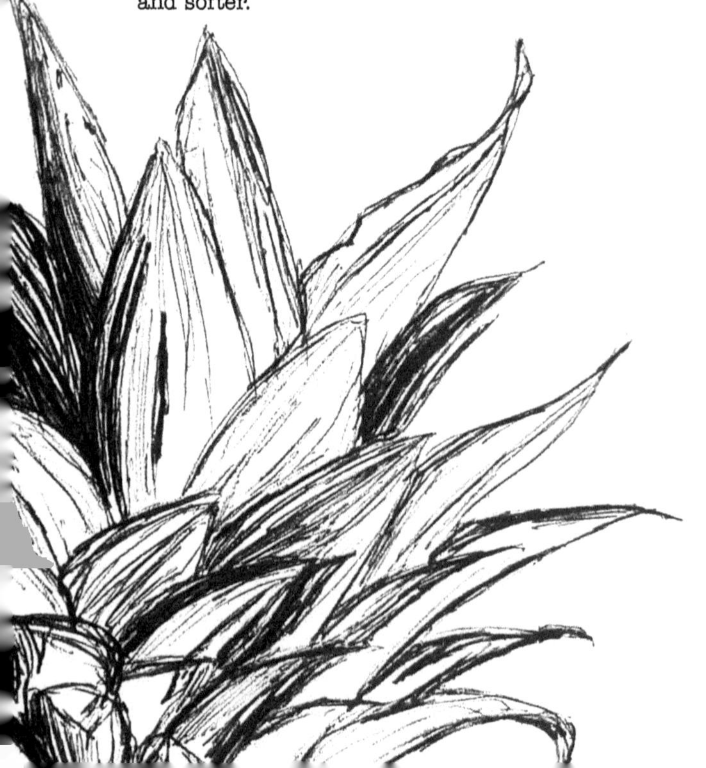

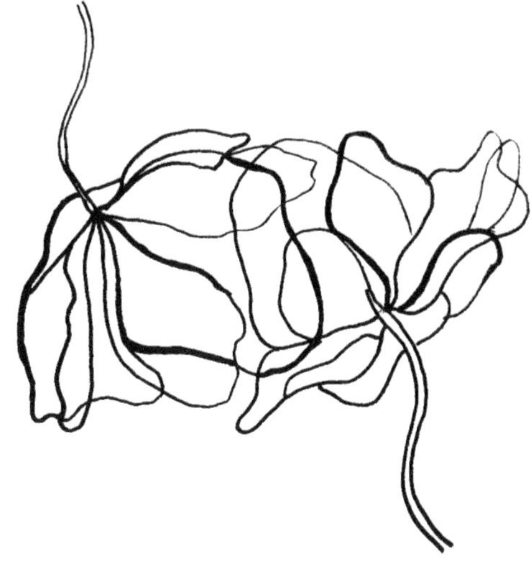

Sand granules

All the sugary, sugary
sugar cane in the world,
pink and purple parted bud flowers,
ghee candles with flickering flames.

A cold bright orange
blue Bay beach coconut
sliced in half,
spicy fried noodles with shrimp.

An icy Phoenix,
the hip swaying attitude
waist dipping of the Island music
flowing over the golden sand granules
warm to touch on the toes.

Warm beach shores,
children playing in the streets,
laughing licking red devils,
red ice.

Weathered palm trees bow in the wind,
sun beating down,
humidity containing this bubble.

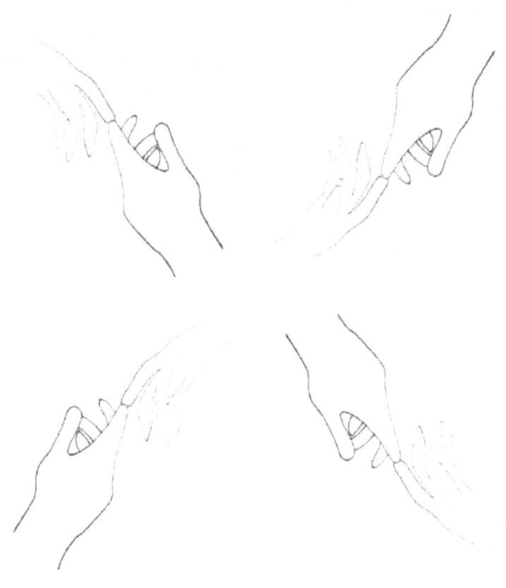

Strangers

Isn't human nature funny ?
Someone who was once a complete stranger
can become
someone who means more
than life to us.
To love,
to trust,
to cry and share,
are all gifts given to us
because people matter.
To be human
is to love people,
who begin as nothing
but strangers.

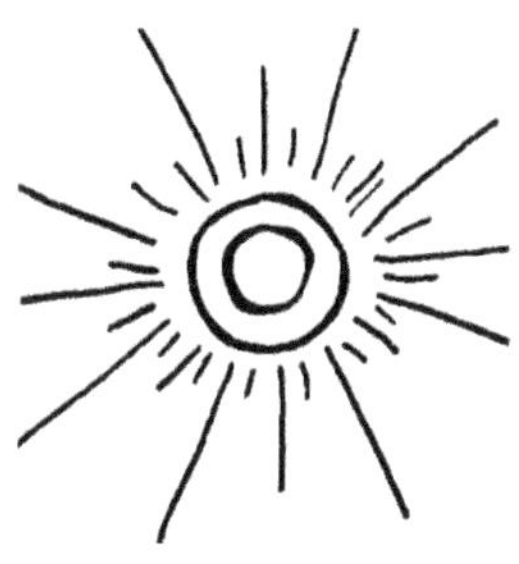

Skipping through the rain

barefoot

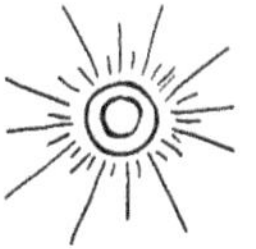

sun beating on our backs

and daze in our eye,

its only 4AM.

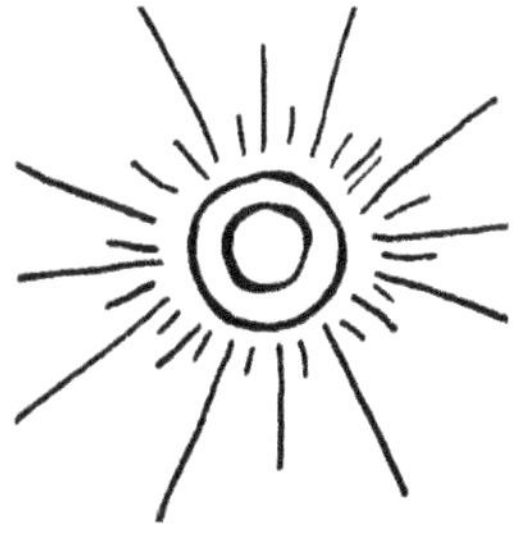

Life is so fragile.
Hold onto people.
Tell them you love them.

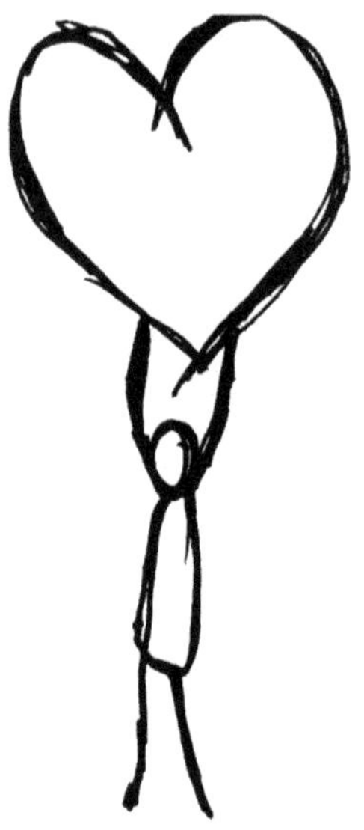

They say we all need a belief
system,
some kind of psychological
anchor. I choose you.
You are my belief system.

I'm having a hard time.
Just let me know
if you understand.

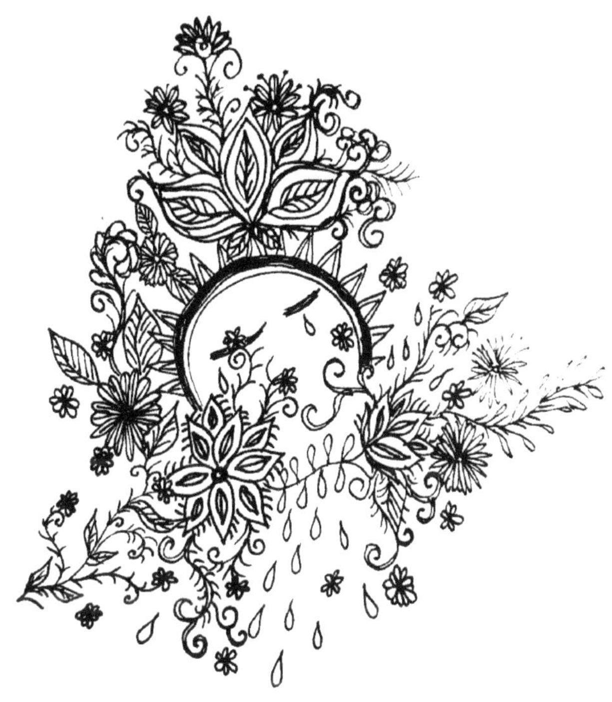

Passage across the opium waters

The floral headdress
rained tears of salt water
bound by the opium sea
and black rivers carrying
those indentured to eternity
in closed promises
of safe passage.

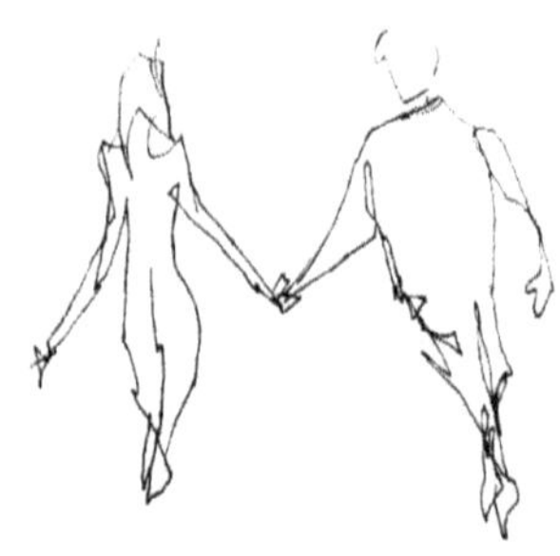

I used to think who would want such an ordinary life,
but I think I'm gradually learning that in times of
desperation,
simplicity can be a saving grace.
Happiness seems to come from the simplest of things.

It is easy to love someone great,
but when that greatness is stripped away
and we see what is left,
the scars, the mistakes and bruises that carve our
stories,
do you love the bare bones that remain ?

I am comfortable with your truth,
every blush punch and drunken mistake,
every time you treated me with coldness.
I am comfortable with my mess,
with the mess I made of our situation.
And if you want,
I 'll always have my hand extended to yours.
Because you are my best friend
and I love you.
I'll always love you.

When the sun touches my face and warms my skin I
will smile and know
that what is meant for me will never
surpass me.
And all I have lost
including you
becomes part of my story.

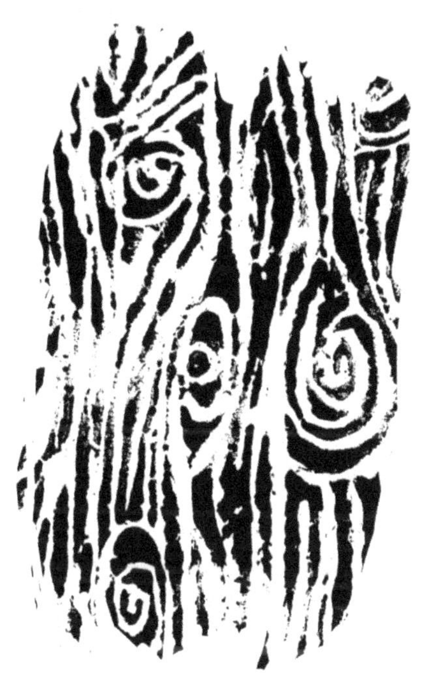

Underground love.

Our fingertips smell like metal
and our breath like the dusty tracks,
as we ride the tube
late into the frosty night,
smiling at each other
as we grip onto the cold
hand rails.

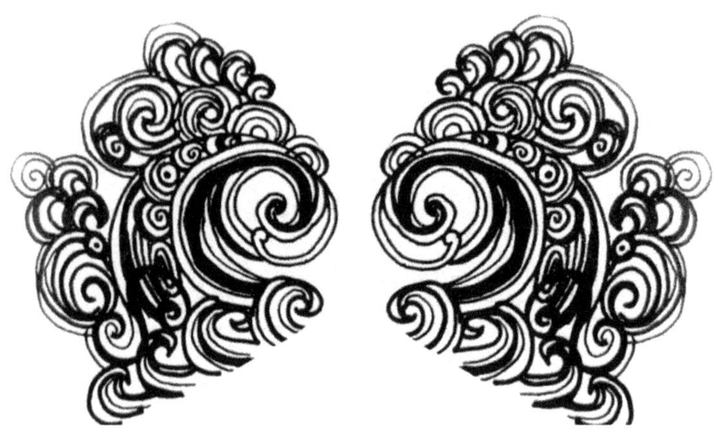

Foundations

Let the rain fall and the paint peel
for when the roots are strong
the foundation will never break.

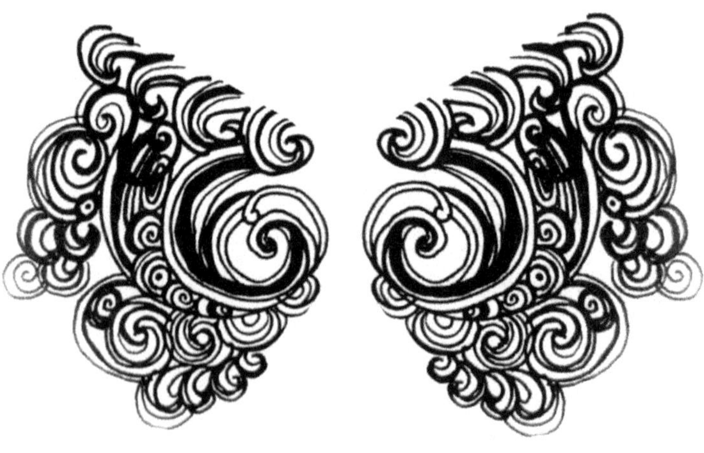

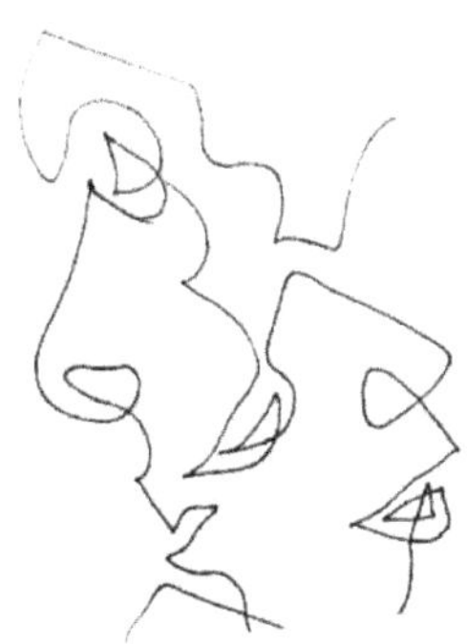

Run

Leave the change on the counter.
Leave the cigarette
in your mouth,
pack a t-shirt dear
and that photo of us,
we will leave this place
behind hand in hand,
with nothing that can lead them
back to us.

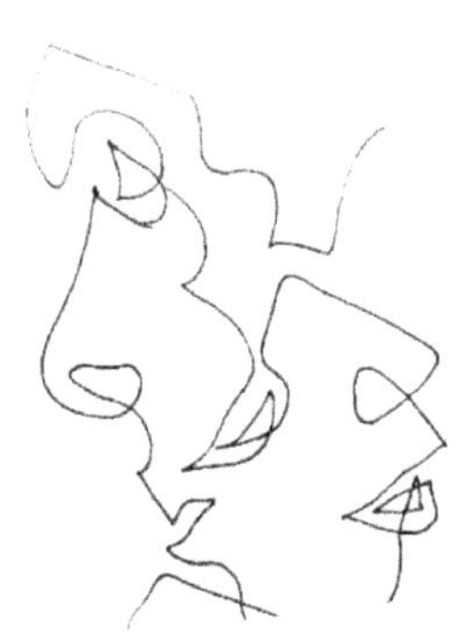

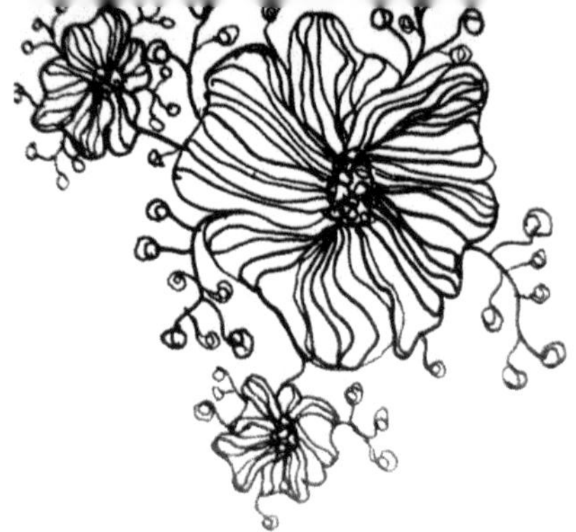

Roots

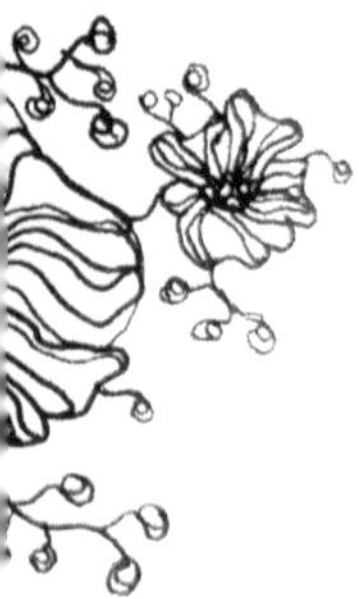

I promise to love all of you dear,
all the tangled messy roots,
all the dirt and ugliness,
because that sweet heart of yours
has me now and forever.
We may not be bound by blood
or thick black ink,
but the seeds which were sown
have bloomed
flowers within me,
and deep set roots
which would take a lifetime
to untangle.
Please be kind to yourself
for the world has no one
with a heart
as sweet and flowery as you.

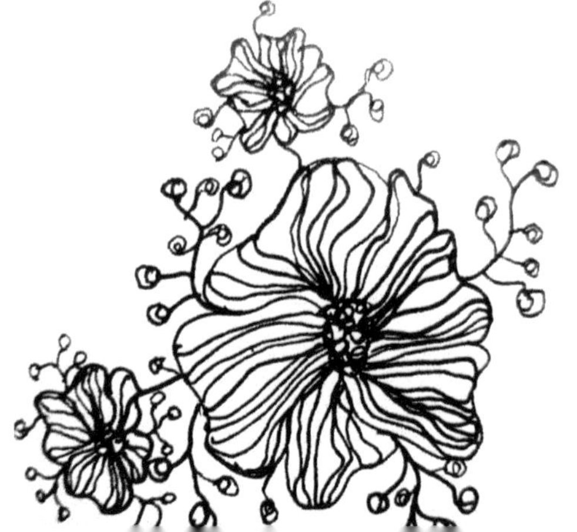

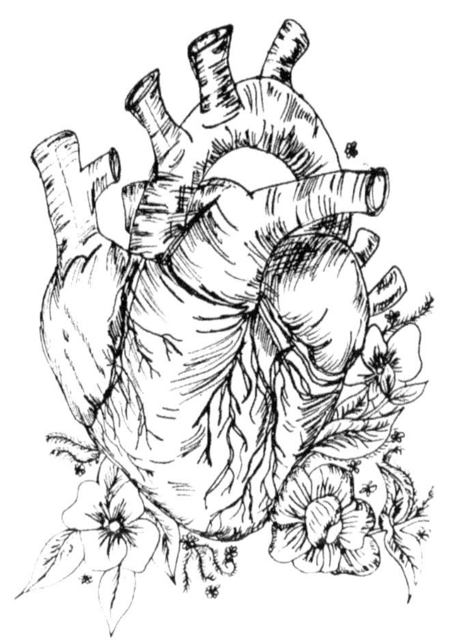

Aorta

You are soft enough
to be pierced and stopped in an instant
by my sharp words and careless actions.
Yet you are strong enough to last a lifetime,
and sometimes there after.
I'll try to be kinder to it.

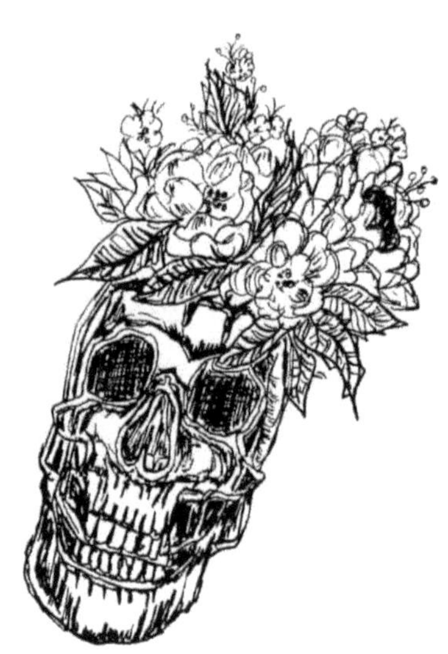

Lessons

The heart has its own mind.
Sometimes
it makes no sense in its urges
to plant seeds where there is no sun.
Regardless of whether or not it succeeds
in its conquests,
that seed will always bloom
a flower, that changes the heart
for the better.

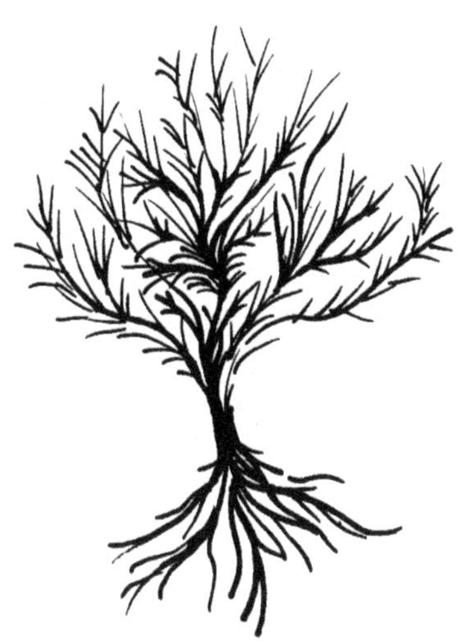

Ancient soul

The soul was like the bark of a tree.
It was hard and rigid,
but carved and complex.
Shaped by disasters
and saved by waters
delivered through storms.
It was deep and scarred,
yet beautiful,
and home to many smaller
and more vulnerable.

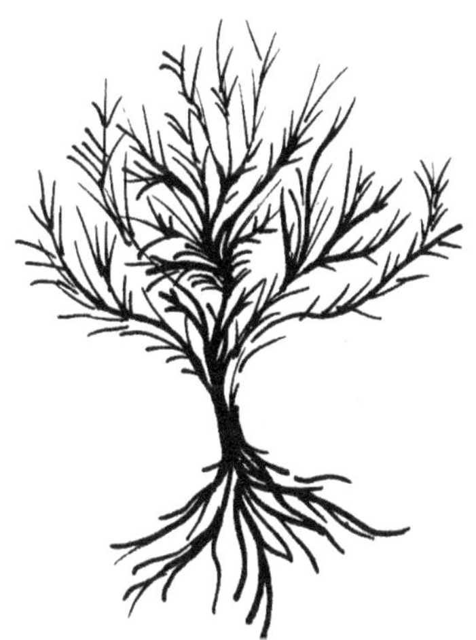

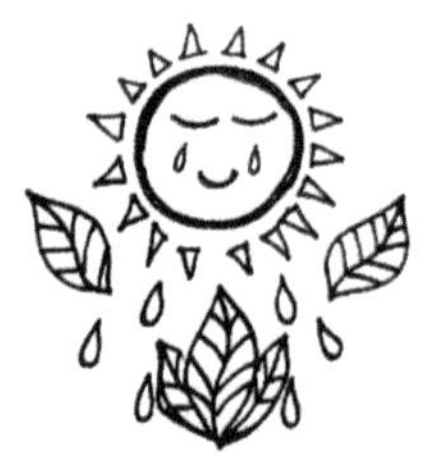

Ripples

It comes in ripples.
Not soft like twilight rings,
tiny pebbles skimmed
on cold mornings at dawn,
but harsh like the instancy
of rock salt hail,
unexpected downpour waterfall
pavement shore.
The ripples just appear.
They bound you.
Surround you
yet you somehow feel as if you are floating.
But still it comes in ripples.
Fingers numb and cold rummage for the house key.
Whatever the art about trauma,
whether it be the watery word,
the attack to the canvas,
the manipulation of our auditory senses,
you can only write about trauma once it has passed,
once the traumatic moment has ended.
There is dislocation and healing
woven into any art about trauma.
Turn the key.
No sensation, the hail keeps pouring down.
The cold keeps engulfing.
Still, one thing there is certainty about is that is comes in
ripples.

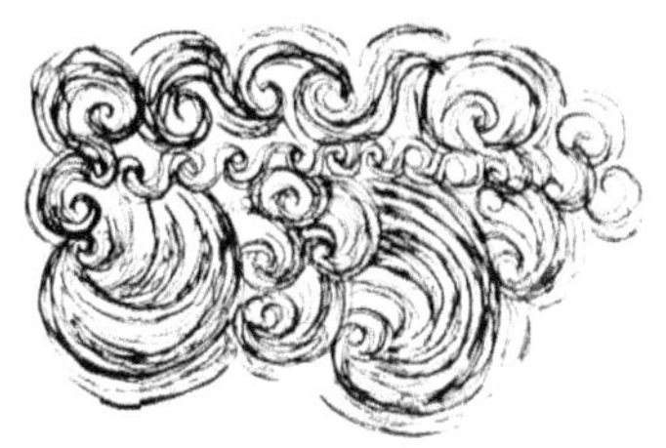

Organic street art.

Pools of cold market water
run
down
tiles of concrete,

meandering
through
cracks in the pavement

and vegetable
peelings
forming grey
paintings on the market floor.
Its beauty,
obvious.
But its
concentration of dirt
and crowd convince us otherwise.
As a result, it becomes
something dirty and overlooked,
avoided and ignored.

I believe the human condition
is somewhat similar.

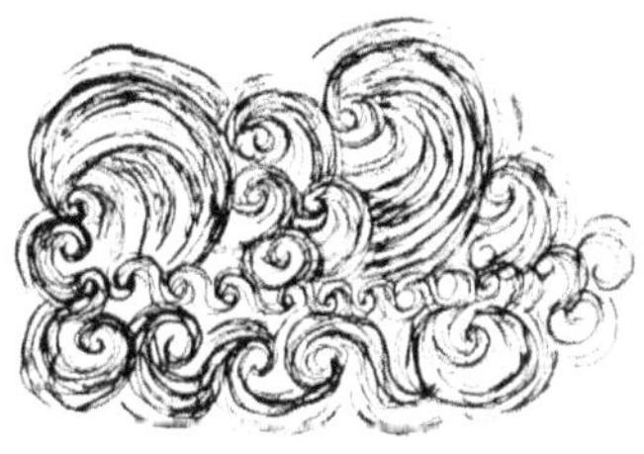

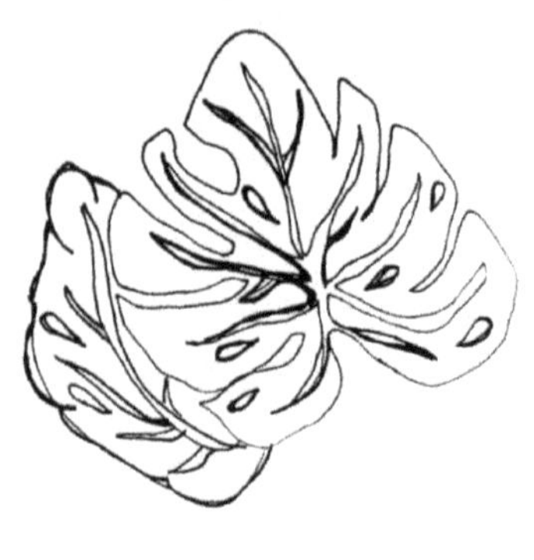

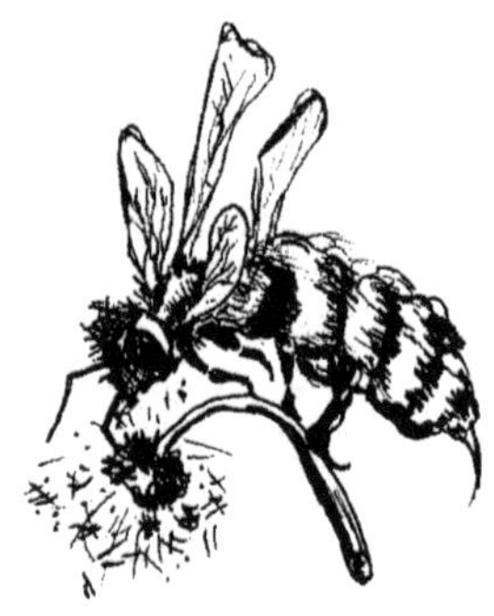

Breeze

Leave it to the

                              breeze,
the sun
                and the trees,

they know what they are doing my love.

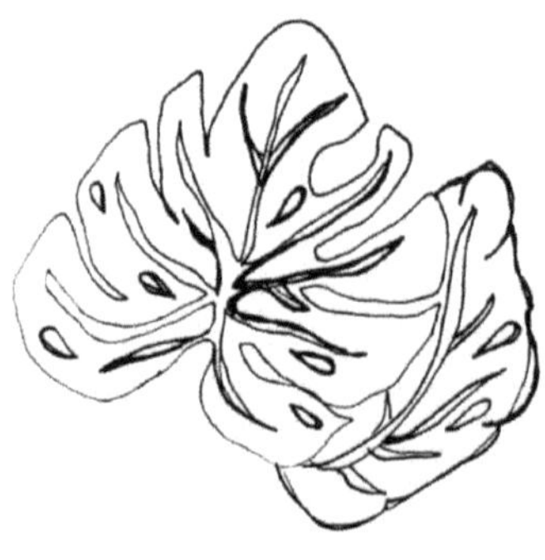

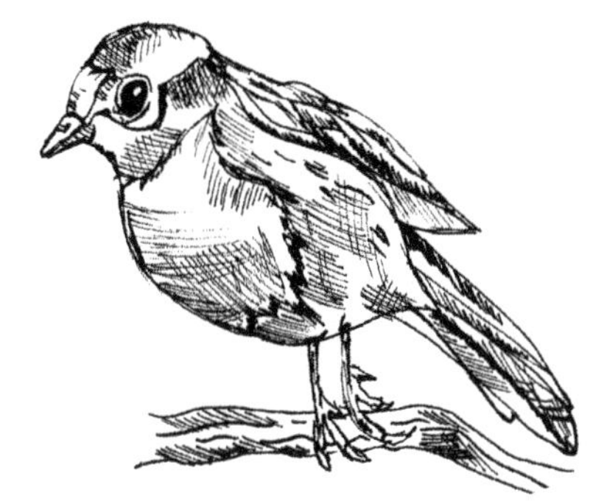

Desk

Rocks from each corner I have visited
sit on my desk at home,
a black metal pot
with a few pens and blunt pencils,
a sketch book with random unfinished lined creations,
pictures of us laughing,
chewy gummy hair tie shaped like a spring,
printed out hologram card of Frida Kahlo,
my old sixth form ID, make up removal pads,
elephant idol that smells like lavender incense
and ash burnt rice,
old worksheets I convince myself I might still need, ink stains
and impulse doodles of lady birds,
coffee rings and plastic straw wrappers
from black bean milk,
a broken zip, navy blue,
I have no idea where that is from,
there are gold sweet wrappers from toffees I eat
to remind me of you,
canisters,
a half eaten packet of sweet coconut oil fried
banana chips, miscellaneous charger cables,
a poem, my favourite, makes me sad,
old earphones with one blown out ear plug
twisted wires, my passport and bus pass.
My desk is scattered with all these things that make up my life.
It's a bitter sweet space.

My God, it was beautiful.

It would take a long time to explain what happened here,
but my God it was beautiful.

The shedding of unnoticed tears breaks my heart,
because it is what I spent so long doing.

Sometimes the thought of you enters my mind,
just for a brief second,
and I'm reminded of how beautiful you made my life.

In the salt water shed for you was my love,
my friendship, tears, concern, hand, laughter
and mind.

I'll always love you, and that's okay.

I'll
pour a little water and act like we never met.

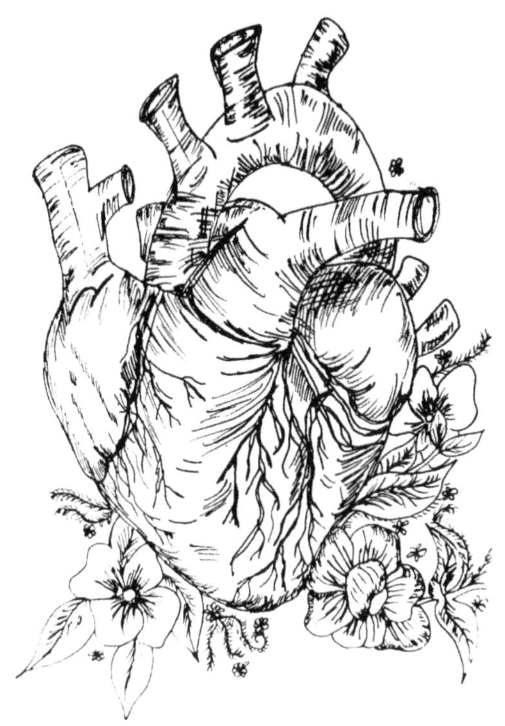

Sow

You planted the seeds within me,
nurtured them enough to let them bloom,
but when the flower petals were ready to bask
in the sun
you plucked the roots out of the flesh
and let me bleed.

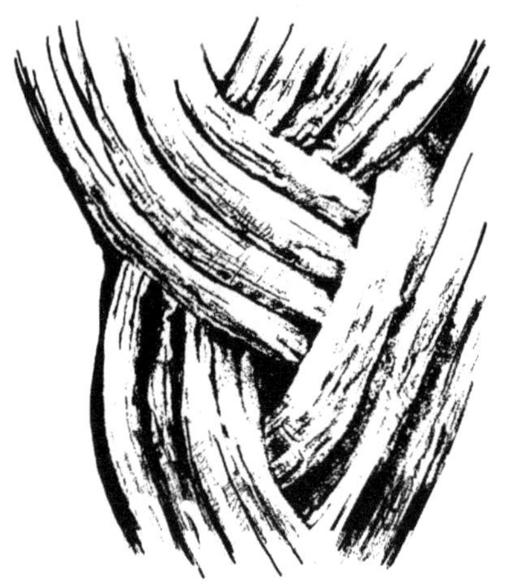

Ropes

You are frayed
and rough
but still
have a heart soft
enough
to want to hold us all together.

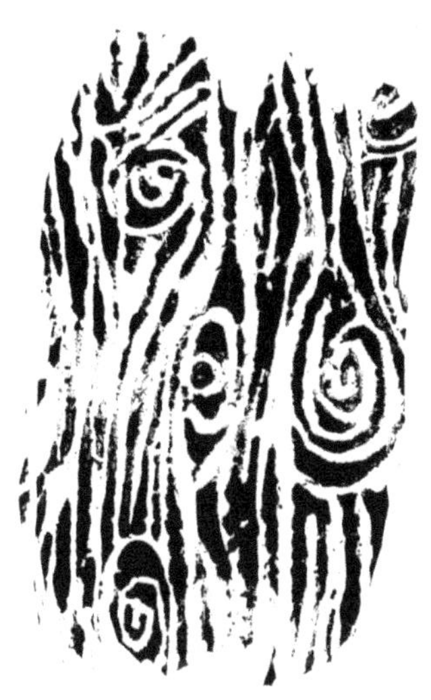

Life lines

If you are not in my destiny
I shall take a knife
and change
the grooves of my palm.

My love is turning into devotion,
I worship you,
the ground you walk on is my home.

You will forever be the poison I pick.

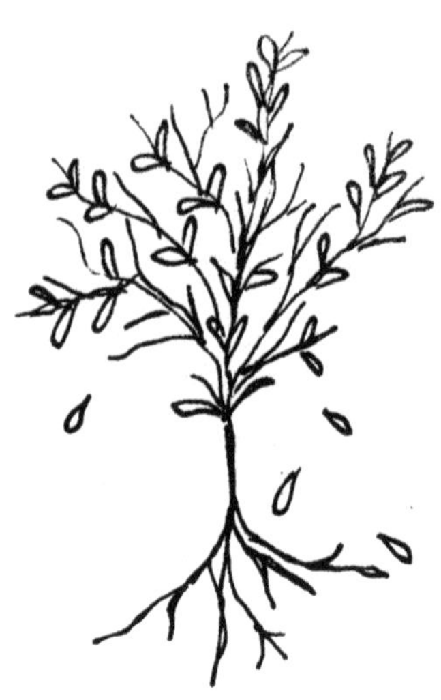

How potently our history informs our present.

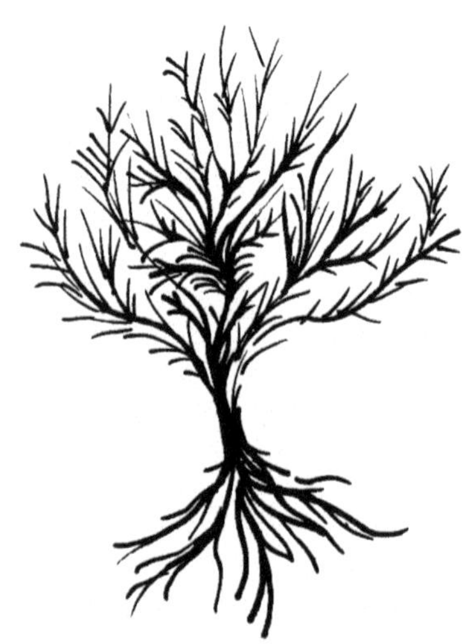

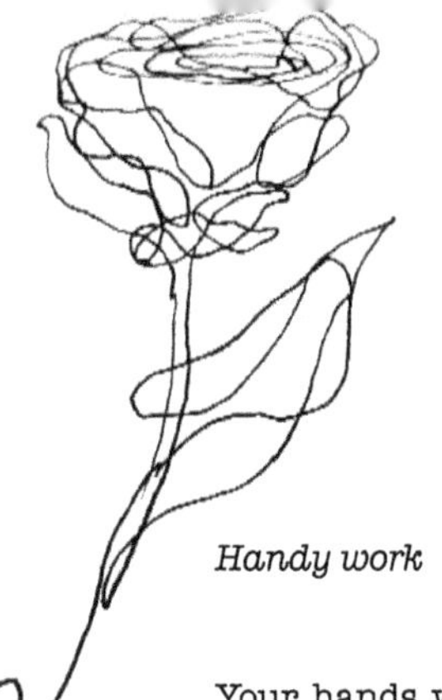

Handy work

Your hands were big,
soft yet still a little rough.
They said you looked older than me,
I liked it.
Short nail buds and cinnamon skin,
small dotted pores and side smudge ink stains
from the fountain pen you write with.
You sneak ideas in your journal
when I am not looking.

Like a line drawing
the more I stare at our story,
the more I give meaning to strokes and dents
that were simply made by accident.

There is something so familiar
yet completely detached about you.
I guess it's my fault.
I let myself love you.

Everything about you, every tiny detail,
every happiness and pain
you shared with me.
Your hands were big, soft yet still a little rough.
They said I could do better.
I am beginning to realise
they were right.

The mask you wear is okay with me,
but know
I wish to learn who you are without it.
I have seen glimmers of your true form.
Yellow flowers swimming in pink light.
And my God it's beautiful.

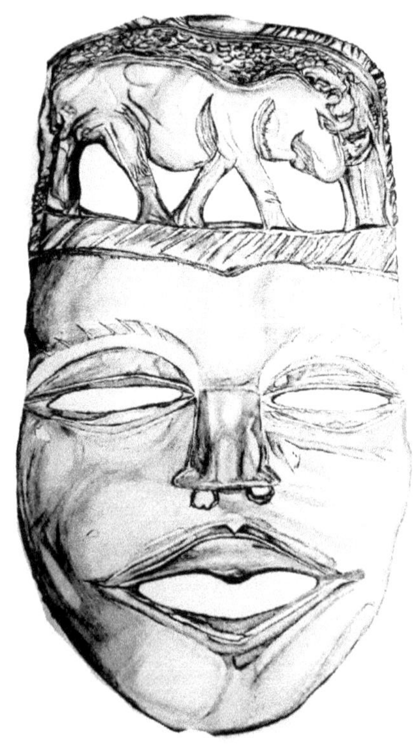

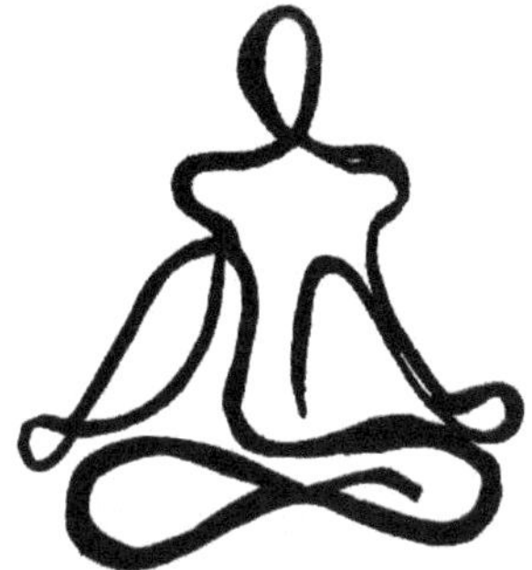

Mantra

Transcend ego and embrace love.

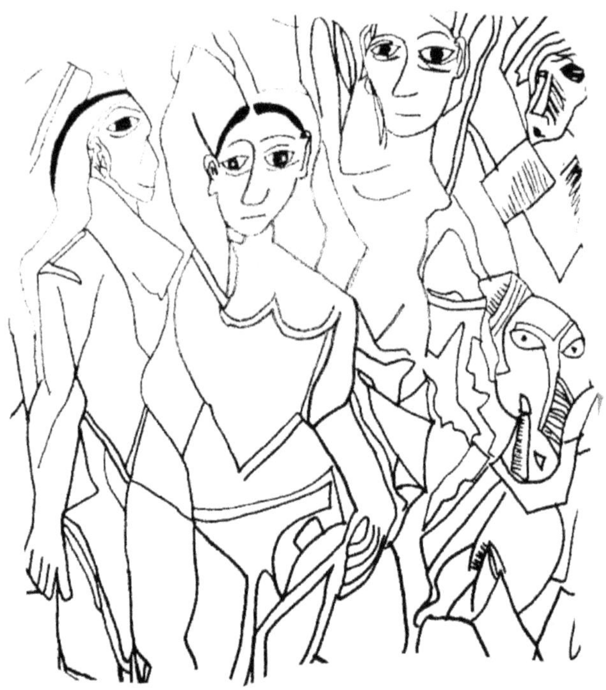

Woman

My, my take a step back
and look at how precious
you are to all of us.

I am in awe of you.
Your mind thinks in a way
that sees not the machinery of the body
but the beauty of the soul.

You made me realise
that it is okay to bring the burning sun
in the mind and heart
back down to earth
every now and again.

Go with light and love.

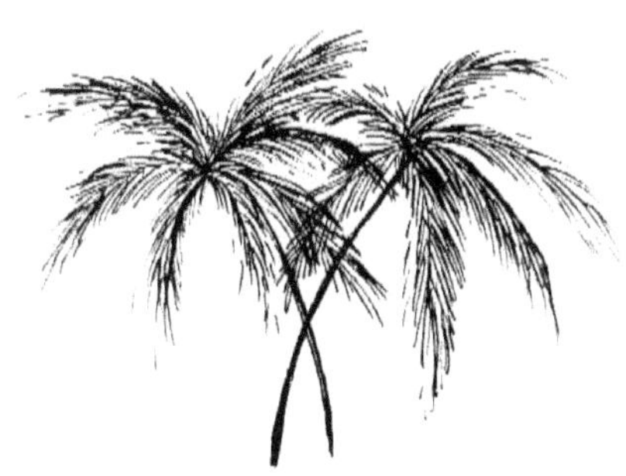

Kiss not spit

Give love to each other.
So often our brothers and sisters collect the paper and
compete,
saliva is used to spit instead of kiss.
No more, my island family, join hands, join in love.
My love.
Extend
        a hand and
deliver a
                        soft touch,
caress
with kind words,

act with compassion,
smile and
breathe   in and out.
Touch your sugar cane hair.
Hug
each other,
kiss one another,
sing,
laugh and eat.
Live life with love
                              in one's heart,
forgive

                  and spread light,

It is free and the greatest gift of all.

Lightning Source UK Ltd.
Milton Keynes UK
UKHW021015210820
368606UK00012B/1069